Golfing Giant

Phil Kettle
illustrated by Craig Smith

Black Hills

Distributed in
the United States of America
by Pacific Learning
P.O. Box 2723
Huntington Beach, CA
92647-0723

Website:
www.pacificlearning.com

Published by Black Hills
(an imprint of Toocool Rules
Pty Ltd)
PO Box 2073
Fitzroy MDC VIC 3065
Australia
61+3+9419-9406

First published in the United States by Black Hills in 2004.
American editorial by Pacific Learning in 2004.
Text copyright © Phillip Kettle, 2002.
Illustration copyright © Toocool Rules Pty Limited, 2002.

 a black dog and Springhill book

Printed in China through Colorcraft Ltd, Hong Kong

ISBN 1 920924 06 X
PL-6206

10 9 8 7 6 5 4 3 2 1   08 07 06 05 04

Contents

Bert

Toocool

Chapter 1
A Perfect Swing

My feet were in the correct position. I looked up at the green, then back at the ball. My swing was perfect.

What a shot!

Or was it?

The ball drifted to the right. It hit the wall. A small chunk of plaster fell out.

The ball shot to the left. CRASH!

Dog ran for the door.

The vase came crashing down in slow motion.

My heart was pounding like a jackhammer.

The sound of breaking
china was always loud—but
never as loud as Mom's voice.

"Toocool! How many times
have I told you not to play
golf inside? Take those clubs
and go outside."

I didn't need to be told twice. I was out of there.

Mom never understood. I kept telling her I had to practice. Practice makes perfect.

I had been planning to ask if I could stay home from school to practice my golf game.

I decided to ask later.

Chapter 2

Chickens and Mud

Outside, the U.S. Open golf tournament was just starting. I tipped my hat to the crowd.

I stuck the tee in the ground and placed the ball on it. I took out the one wood.

I wound up and whacked the ball.

The ball disappeared up the fairway.

Then, at the last minute, a gust of wind blew it off course.

It hit the roof of the toolshed and rolled along the gutter. It fell into the downspout and plopped in the mud.

This was going to be tricky. I had to get the ball out of the mud and into a better position.

I walked along the fairway toward the ball.

Bert the Rooster saw me coming. He saw the golf club in my hand. His eyes practically popped out of his head. He looked terrified. I could not figure out why.

He took off for the chicken coop.

The hens saw him coming. They all started screeching. The chicken coop sounded like a car full of clowns. I ignored the noise.

I was a golfing giant. We always stay focused.

I studied the ball. I had to make it go around the back of the toolshed, past the lemon tree, and over Dog's house.

This would take the seven iron. Whack!

The ball clipped the side of the shed, then flew into Dog's house. It bounced around inside his house.

Luckily, Dog was under my house at the time.

The ball rolled out and landed in Dog's water bowl.

Great shot! The crowd burst into applause. All the cameras were on me. I hoped I didn't have mud in my hair.

I smiled and got ready for my next shot.

Chapter 3

The Chip Shot

I had to drive the ball so that it went through the back door of the garage and out the front door—another difficult shot.

From there, it was a simple chip shot to the pin near the clubhouse.

I stood back. I studied the shot. I put the seven iron back and took out the one wood.

Whack! The ball sailed through the back door of the garage.

As it turned out, the shot was a little off. It was not up to my usual standard.

I yelled, "Fore!"

It was too late.

The ball slammed into the brick wall. Then it rebounded onto the workbench.

Wood and tools and paint went everywhere.

The ball rolled slowly out the front door of the garage.

It was no longer white. It was sort of rainbow colorcd.

It lurched across the grass and stopped under a rosebush.

Luckily, I had my special foot club. A gentle tap and the ball was back in play.

I looked at the scoreboard. I was still in the lead, but I needed to make sure that I scored well from now on.

I was ready for the chip shot. The nine iron was the club to use.

I practiced my swing.

My fans got quiet. They could feel the pressure.

I wiped the sweat from my brow.

I chipped the ball.

The ball sailed through the air. It dropped ten feet from the hole, then rolled right in!

It was a fantastic shot!

The crowd went wild. I had jumped to a two-shot lead!

Mom heard me cheering.
She came running outside.
I thought she was coming to
check my score.

"Toocool! Stay away from the house! You should be putting, not swinging."

The pressure of the U.S. Open must have been too much for Mom. She looked tired. She went back into the clubhouse for a cup of coffee.

Chapter 4
The Last **Hole**

It was the last hole of the U.S. Open. I had a two-shot lead. This was the most difficult part of the course.

The fairway went across the back of the clubhouse. The green ran along the side of the clubhouse patio.

This hole normally required two shots—just to get the ball to the green.

I was sure I could get it there with one shot.

It was worth the risk.

I pulled out the three iron. I put my feet in the correct spot and wiggled my hips—just like the golfers do on TV.

I lined up the ball. It made a whistling sound as I hit it.

I wanted the ball to hit the tree and turn onto the green.

That was where my plan fell apart.

The ball flew from the tree. It had gathered speed. It had gathered force.

Instead of flying along the side of the patio, it went right through the clubhouse window.

The sound of breaking glass sent a shiver down my spine. I would need plenty of prize money to fix that.

Chapter 5
Time to Leave

The clubhouse door flew open.
This is when I decided to
leave. I could always get my
trophy later.

I dropped the golf clubs
and dove under the house.

Dog was still there. He
looked at me. I thought
I heard him laugh. Maybe it
was a cough. I was not sure.

I could hear Mom loud
and clear.

"Toocool! Come here
this instant!"

I knew she did not want to give me my trophy. She had something else in mind.

I decided to stay under the house for a while.

I needed time to think about how well I had played in the U.S. Open.

All golfing giants need time to think—especially when it's almost football season.

The End!

Toocool's
Golf Glossary

Chip shot—A short shot to get the golf ball onto the green.

Fairway—The part of the golf course between the tees and the putting greens. The grass on the fairway is kept short so the ball doesn't get stuck when you try to hit it.

Pin—The flagpole that shows you where the hole is.

Tee—A small plastic or wood object. At the beginning of each hole, you stick it in the ground, set the ball on it, then hit the ball off of it.

Toocool's Backyard
Golf Course

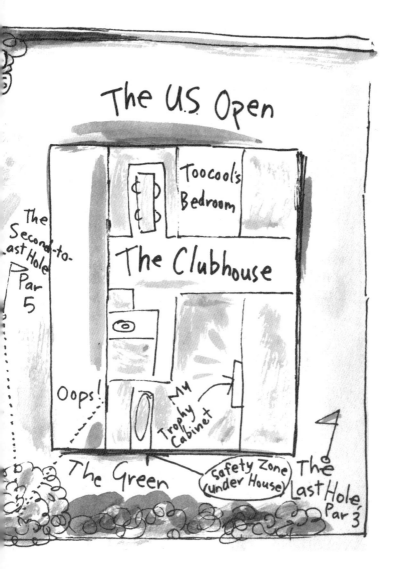

The U.S. Open

Toocool's Bedroom

The Clubhouse

The Second-to-Last Hole
Par 5

Oops!

MY Trophy Cabinet

The Green

Safety Zone (under House)

The Last Hole
Par 3

31

Toocool's Quick Summary
Golf

Golf is a game that is played with a small ball and special stick that is called a golf club.

Players try to hit the ball into holes that are placed around a grass course.

Players have to put up with annoying obstacles called hazards. Some of the hazards are put there on purpose, such as sand traps and little lakes. Other hazards are natural, such as trees and bad weather.

Scoring is based on how many shots it takes you to play all the holes. The fewer hits it takes you, the better. In golf, the person with the lowest score wins!

Most games of golf last for eighteen holes, and that can take all day! If you're in a hurry, you can play nine holes, but even that can take a while. This is especially true if you keep hitting the ball into sand traps and trees—or if you have to stop and explain why your ball went through the clubhouse window.

The Golf Clubs

Contains golf clubs, including seven, nine, and three irons, plus a one wood and a putter.

(and the foot club!)

Ball

Tee

Q & A with Toocool
He Answers His Own Questions

🏐 **How far can golfers hit the ball?**

That depends on what club you use. The lower the number on the golf club, the farther the ball is supposed to go. If you use a one wood, you can hit the ball a long way. If you hit with a nine iron, most times the ball will go high in the air, but not a long way.

Are all golf courses the same?

All golf courses are different. That is what makes golf an interesting game. The best golf course I have played on is the one in my backyard. It has a lot of special hazards, such as the toolshed and the lemon tree. Sometimes, there are moving targets, but I try to avoid them.

What is a birdie?

A birdie is a good score. You have to try to get the ball in the hole in a certain number of shots. The number of shots is called the par. A birdie is when you get the ball in the hole in one shot less than the par.

Have you ever gotten a birdie?

I almost got Bert the Rooster once. Now Bert hides when he sees the golf clubs.

Have you ever gotten a hole in one?

Yes, lots of times. Of course, Dog is the only one who has seen me do it.

What happens if you hit your ball into the lake?

You never see it again, unless there's a drought and the lake dries up.

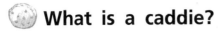 What is a caddie?

A caddie is someone who carries your clubs around for you. A caddie also helps you choose the best club for each shot. Only important golfers have caddies.

Do you have a caddie?

Of course I do. Dog is my caddie. He doesn't carry my clubs though, because he has no idea which club is the best. He does find all my lost balls—not that I lose many balls. I'm too good for that. I'm always in control of my game.

Golf Quiz
How Much Do You Know about Golf?

Q1 What is an air shot?
A. When you swing and miss the ball. **B.** A new ride at the amusement park. **C.** A kind of dance.

Q2 What is a clubhouse?
A. A home for elderly clubs.
B. A place where golfers can rest.
C. A really big sandwich.

Q3 If a golf hole is par three, how many shots are you supposed to take to get the ball in the hole?
A. One. **B.** Two. **C.** Three.

Q4 If you get a birdie, what have you done?

A. Annoyed a rooster. *B.* Put the ball in the hole in one less than par. *C.* Bought a take-out chicken.

Q5 What is a driver?

A. Whoever takes you to play golf. *B.* The person who drives the school bus. *C.* The golf club you use to tee off.

Q6 What is a bad slice?

A. A piece of stale cake.
B. When you try to hit the ball straight, but it curves instead.
C. When you chop out a big chunk of grass with your club.

Q7 What are sand traps?

A. Tight swimming trunks.

B. Peanut butter sandwiches.

C. Big holes on the golf course filled with sand.

 Q8 What is a putter?

A. A golf club you use when your ball is on the green. **B.** A very small motorcycle. **C.** A person who puts things away.

 Q9 What do you yell when you think your ball might hit someone?

A. "Help! Get an ambulance."

B. "Fore!" **C.** "Look out!"

Q10 Who would you ask if you wanted golf lessons?
A. A golf pro. **B.** A caddie.
C. Toocool.

ANSWERS

1 A.   *2* B.   *3* C.
4 B.   *5* C.   *6* B.
7 C.   *8* A.   *9* B.
10 C.

If you got ten questions right, you must have gotten lucky. If you got more than five right, you still don't have a clue about golf. If you got fewer than five right, you could hunt for lost golf balls.

TOOCOOL

Football Legend

It's the end of the season and **Toocool** has led his team to the Super Bowl. Can one fantastic player ensure victory in this high-pressure game?

Titles in the Toocool series